Clara Barton

By Wil Mara

Consultants
Nanci R. Vargus, Ed.D.
Primary Multiage Teacher
Decatur Township Schools, Indianapolis, Indiana

Katharine A. Kane, Reading Specialist
Former Language Arts Coordinator
San Diego County Office of Education

Children's Press ®
A Division of Scholastic Inc.
New York   Toronto   London   Auckland   Sydney
Mexico City   New Delhi   Hong Kong
Danbury, Connecticut

Designer: Herman Adler Design
Photo Researcher: Caroline Anderson
The photo on the cover shows Clara Barton.

Library of Congress Cataloging-in-Publication Data

Mara, Wil.
 Clara Barton / by Wil Mara.
  p. cm. — (Rookie biographies)
 Includes index.
 Summary: An introduction to the life of the nurse who served on the battlefields
 of the Civil War and later founded the American Red Cross.
  ISBN 0-516-22523-5 (lib. bdg.)   0-516-27339-6 (pbk.)
  1. Barton, Clara, 1821-1912—Juvenile literature. 2. Red Cross—United
 States—Biography—Juvenile literature. 3. Nurses—United States—
 Biography—Juvenile literature. [1. Barton, Clara, 1821-1912. 2. Nurses.
 3. Women—Biography.] I. Title. II. Series.
  HV569.B3 M373 2002
  361.7'634'092—dc21

                                2001008316

Do you like to help others?

Clara Barton did. She helped millions of people.

Barton was born in Massachusetts
on December 25, 1821.

When she was eleven, her brother David was hurt after he fell from a barn roof. She took care of him for the next two years until he was better.

In 1861, the Civil (SIV-il) War began in the United States. The northern states fought the southern states.

There were many hurt soldiers during the Civil War. Barton saw hospitals filled with them. She wanted to help them.

Some hotels had to be used as hospitals. Barton even took some soldiers into her own home.

She wrote letters asking for help. People sent more food, clothes, and money, too.

Barton worked in hospitals on the battlefield. A battlefield is a place where a war is fought.

13

Barton was called the "Angel of the Battlefield." The battlefield was a dangerous place. This did not stop Clara Barton from helping hurt soldiers there.

After the war, many soldiers were missing. Families did not know what happened to their loved ones.

Clara Barton looked for these missing soldiers. She found out what happened to nearly 22,000 lost soldiers. Most of them had died.

17

Then Barton went to Europe
(YUR-uhp). She learned about
a group that helped people
in need. It was called the
Red Cross.

19

20

Barton thought the Red Cross should be in America, too. She started the American Red Cross in 1881.

In 1898, there was an explosion on a ship called the *U.S.S. Maine*. Clara Barton and members of the American Red Cross helped the people who were hurt in the explosion.

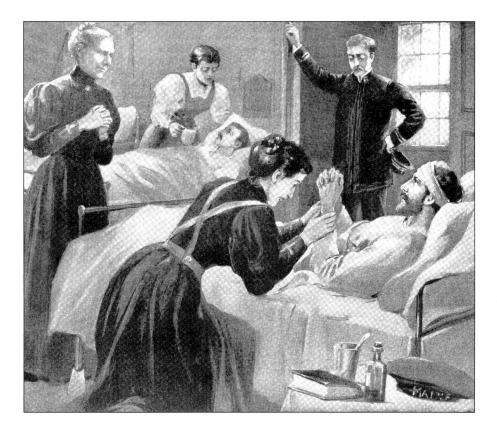

23

On April 12, 1912, Clara Barton died. She was 91 years old.

Today, the American Red Cross
is still helping people in need.

It has helped people during
earthquakes, tornadoes,
hurricanes, and floods.

Clara Barton was called the "Angel of the Battlefield." She was an angel in many other ways, too. She was always ready to help others.

29

Words You Know

American Red Cross

battlefield

Clara Barton

David Barton

help

hospitals

hotel

soldiers

Index

About the Author

Wil Mara has written over fifty books. His works include both fiction and nonfiction for children and adults. He lives with his wife and three daughters in northern New Jersey.

Photo Credits

Photographs © 2002: Brown Brothers: cover, 9, 10, 13, 17, 23, 31 bottom left, 31 top right, 31 bottom right; Clara Barton National Historic Site: 5, 30 bottom left; Corbis Images: 29; Hulton|Archive/Getty Images: 27 (George Eastman House/Lewis W. Hine/Archive Photos), 26; Library of Congress: 6, 7, 14, 20, 30 top left, 30 top right, 30 bottom right; Photo Researchers, NY/Alan D. Carey: 3, 31 top left; The American Red Cross: 24 (Poli), 19.